A
Topsy
-Turvy
History of
New
Orleans
&
Ten Tiny Turtles

300 years and
slowly counting...

Story by Tania Lee and Simone Rathlé
Illustrations by Tania Lee

With thanks to Charlee Williamson
for identifying our noble protagonists

and to the Historic New Orleans Collection
for its kind review of the non-reptilian facts contained herein

To EVA
♡ Nana
+ Papa
2018
XX OO

To all who love New Orleans
this book is warmly dedicated

There have always been turtles in the courtyard
of Brennan's restaurant in New Orleans -- even before
there was a Brennan's restaurant.

They were living there among the native Chitimacha when
Jean-Baptiste LeMoyne de Bienville arrived 300 years ago,
and established a settlement for France.

He named it for the Duke of Orleans,
who was ruling France at the time.

They were there fifty years later,
when the Spanish took control...

... and they were there when the French took it back.

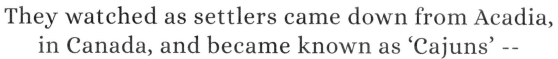

They watched as settlers came down from Acadia,
in Canada, and became known as 'Cajuns' --

NAPOLEON • JEFFERSON

And when the French sold their Louisiana Territory
to the United States of America.

It didn't surprise them that everyone seemed to want to come to New Orleans. Before long, they'd met Africans, and Haitians,

and Italians,

and Germans,

and Irish.

NAPOLEON HOUSE

They wondered, with all
their neighbors, if Napoleon
himself would accept the
mayor's invitation to come
live in their city.
[He did not; he died, instead.]

They were on hand when Andrew Jackson forced back the British at the Battle of New Orleans in 1815, with the help of the notorious pirate, Jean Lafitte. Jackson went on to become our 7th president. Lafitte became a spy, and then disappeared. The turtles? They stayed put.

When 417 Royal Street was
built, they took up residence
in its shaded courtyard.
Early on, the building was
home to the very first bank in
the Louisiana territory.
A secret tunnel was dug deep
below the surface to convey its
gold to safety, in case of pirate
attack. Its exact location is
now lost -- to humans.

The turtles were pleased to help a later resident with his chess game.
His name was Paul Morphy, and he went on to become the
unofficial world champion.

The French families of New Orleans had always observed their ancient Catholic traditions with great reverence. In 1857, things got a little more lively.

That was when the very first Mardi Gras procession was held,
with marching bands and rolling floats, and the turtles have welcomed
the annual festivities ever since.

They survived the plagues of Yellow Fever and Influenza that carried away many of their human neighbors.

They were jubilant when jazz erupted in their beloved French Quarter, and carried the spirit of New Orleans around the world.

In 1955, the Brennan family transformed the turtles' lovely pink house into a restaurant called Brennan's. Turns out they were naturals at hospitality.

So were the waiters, the maître d', the cooks,
the dishwashers, the bakers, and the bartenders.

One August, a mighty storm named Katrina washed
the turtles clear out of the French Quarter.

They returned to a thoroughly topsy-turvy courtyard.

Times were tough,
but the turtles were tougher.
The determined family began
rebuilding its little corner of
the world. It was slow going.
Imagine the new owners'
surprise when they
discovered them there
in the sun!

The turtles were sent
off for a relaxing holiday
in the backyard of
Chef Haley. They were
glad to get away.

She was glad to have them.

Their triumphant return to the courtyard was marked with a festive parade, which is now an annual event.

In the interest of time, the guests of honor are given a lift.

There is a strong family resemblance among the turtles,
and to help their friends tell them apart, they've adopted the
names of the five Mother Sauces of classic French cuisine,

together with five other sauces
that add further glory to New Orleans cooking.
That makes ten.

Their courtyard is better than ever,
ideal for a large family of swimmers and sunbathers.

The turtles still take great pride in greeting guests and being generally helpful around the restaurant. As you would expect, they have especially good table manners.

Today, if you come to Brennan's, look for the turtles in the fountain in the courtyard. Be sure to stop and say hello. They've seen a whole lot of New Orleans history, and they'll be awfully glad to see *you*.

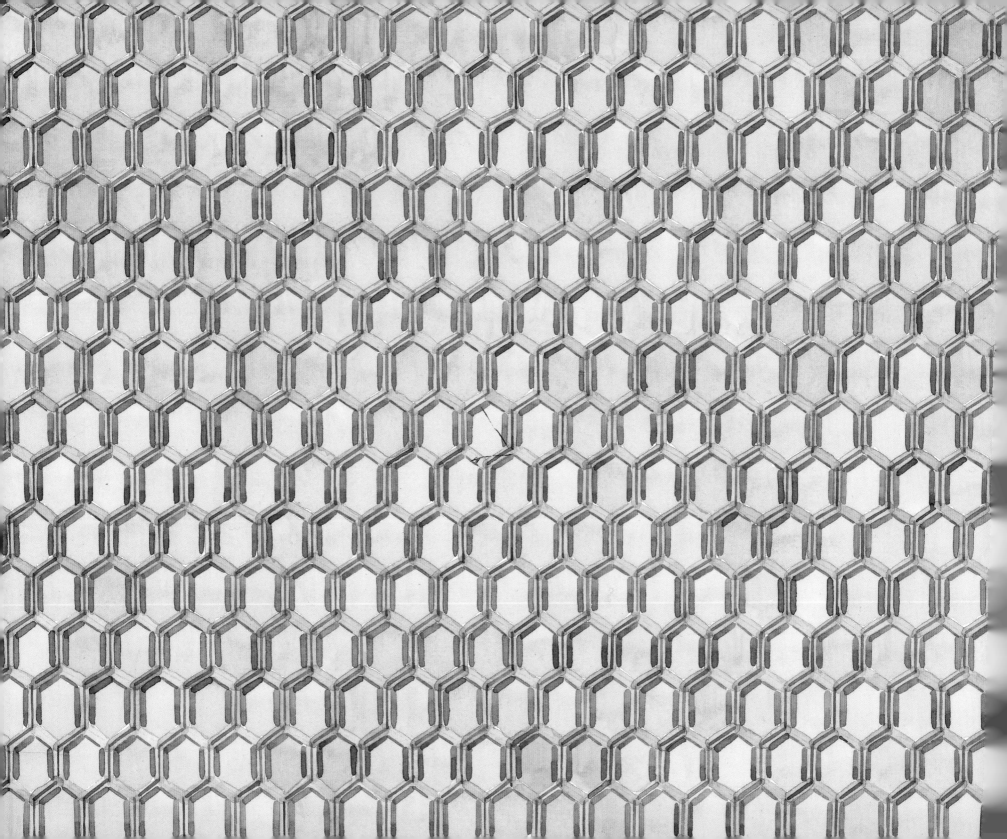